THEN & NOW

NORCROSS

Opposite: This group of young men, self-described as "the Depot Gang," would race their muscle cars, no Chevys allowed, up and down Highway 141 about a mile from the center of town, mostly because there was not much else to do. After dark, the dirt road was relatively safe for this practice, but now that road is paved, with four lanes of nonstop traffic. (Courtesy of Carl and Joan Garner.)

THEN & NOW

NORCROSS

Sally Toole and
Kate Awtrey

I dedicate this project to my sweet and supportive husband, Mark, for enthusiastically tagging along to snap or scan pictures and speak to folks about their life stories. I honor the memory of my dad, Bill Hirsch, a true fan of all things golf, who appears on page 63. —Sally Toole

I dedicate the photographs in this book to my mom and dad, my brother, John, and my Mamaw and PawPaw. Thank you to Charlotte B. Teagle, the Annie Leibovitz of my five-year-old world, who inspired me to always have a camera in hand, and to David Tulis, who believed in me even when I did not believe in myself. —Kate Awtrey

ISBN 978-0-7385-9138-4

Library of Congress Control Number: 2011938563

Published by Arcadia Publishing
Charleston, South Carolina

Printed in the United States of America

For all general information, please contact Arcadia Publishing:
Telephone 843-853-2070
Fax 843-853-0044
E-mail sales@arcadiapublishing.com

Visit us on the Internet at www.arcadiapublishing.com

On the Front Cover: "The Depot Gang" included, from left to right, Allen Cawley, Hilton Johnson, Tommy Cape, George Doby, Hubert Terrell, B.R. Corn, Lane Campbell, Dodger DeLeon, Harold Garmon, Billy McGinnis, Tommy Herren, and Carl Garner. Now seasoned car buffs, the gang began the annual Norcross Car Show, an event that brings thousands to town each May and awards scholarships to local medical students. The depot appears then and now. (Then image courtesy of Carl and Joan Garner; now image courtesy of Kate Awtrey.)

On the Back Cover: In the 1890s, Confederate veterans hold a reunion on the Medlock Hotel's porch. (Courtesy of Evelyn Norman.)

Contents

ACKNOWLEDGMENTS

For sharing their personal pictures, stories, and homes, the authors wish to thank Evelyn "Bud" Norman and her son, Bill Norman; the Nesbit family; Carl and Joan Garner; Rufus Dunnigan; Hattie McLendon; David Jackson; Greg Jackson Studios; Betty Sprull; Lily Toole; the Adams family; Clifton "Buddy" Ray; Jeff Costello; Michelle Morgan; James Wingo; Ann and Jerry Brown; Jennifer Holwill and her father, Anthony Holwill; Bob Warbington; Gordon Tomlinson, attorney; Sherry and Carl Johnson, a wonderful couple who literally saved this project; and the Bolton family. Also, thanks to the Norcross Old Timers Baseball Association; the Gwinnett Historical Society; the Gwinnett History Museum; Mizuno Sports Equipment; Norcross Scout Troop 26; Norcross First Baptist Church; Norcross First Methodist Church; the Lionheart Theatre Company; Taylor Covert of Home Shop; History Walks of Norcross; Randy and Tammy Johnson of Woods Animal Hospital; the Bleu House Market and Café; the City of Norcross; Anne LeBaire of Kudzu Art Zone; John Landstrom of the Blue Moon Cycle Shop; and most especially, Cate Kitchen, the director of the welcome center; the wait staff of Paizanos; and the 45 South Café for keeping us caffeinated and well-fed while working in cozy corners of their establishments hour after hour.

The authors attribute NorcrossPatch.com editor Laura Sullivan and Dr. Seuss for bringing them together. Posthumously, the authors appreciate John and Martha Miller Adams, Anita Andrews, Avery Graves, Martha Simpson Nesbit, Fran Nesbit Fickling, and Garland Sexton. Unless otherwise noted, the vintage "then" images are credited to those aforementioned friends and neighbors or they are from the personal collection of Sally Toole. All the modern "now" images, unless otherwise noted, were snapped from behind the talented viewfinder of Kate Awtrey.

Introduction

Early settlers, winning their land in the lottery of 1820, traded and mingled peacefully with the Creek and Cherokee living in the four original settlements in and around what would become Norcross. The Native Americans hunted, lived, buried their dead, and coursed trails across what now is considered Hall, Habersham, Walton, and Gwinnett Counties.

In the 1860s, volunteer regiments, most notably the Flint Hill Grays, were sponsored by the earliest settlers, who struggled to hold onto their States' Rights and hold back northern aggression. The Grays' uniforms were hand-stitched by a ladies' Sunday School group of the first primitive Methodist church, a structure no longer standing. Tucked in that area is a crumbling graveyard full of stones that mark dates from the early 1800s, well before Norcross was established on October 26, 1870.

Men and boys returning from the Civil War found their families splintered, their farms ravaged, and their businesses in ruins. It was during this reconstructive era that Jonathan Thrasher, an Atlanta businessman privy to some inside railroad information, purchased Land Lot No. 254 from a Mr. Wilson. The lot was 180 acres around the site where the Richmond-Danville Railroad planned to end a commuter route, 20 miles north of Atlanta. That plat now encompasses the historic section of Norcross, the entirety of which is listed in the National Register of Historic Places.

Thrasher and others felled and milled timber for the railroad ties running northward, upon which rails were laid for a commuter line called the Airline Belle. So began the little railroad town of Norcross, named for Thrasher's friend and the fourth mayor of Atlanta, Jonathan Norcross. Thrasher divided the lots, auctioning off some to businessmen and giving away some for the construction of multiuse buildings, which the community could use for church services, a mixed grade school, and Masonic lodge meetings on an upper floor.

From the late 1800s to the Great Depression, Norcross was promoted as "Atlanta's Favorite Summer Resort" and went through a boom. The quaint downtown enjoys an abundant canopy of trees and fresh air, a result of its high elevation along the eastern continental divide. It is reported in the book *Norcross*, by Irene Ewing Crapo and Martha Miller Adams, that an extravagant write-up was produced by the chamber of commerce in the 1890s promoting the town as being "The most favored spot on the face of the earth with a translucent air invigorating every breath providing freedom from the danger of malarious disease giving visitors freedom from the danger of yellow fever." This pamphlet, written by W. Oscar Groce, goes on to tout the town as a "Heaven favored region believing visitors' health and strength will return here." Groce credits local physician and former Confederate surgeon Dr. Moses Richardson as "one of the oldest and ablest in this section," and reports that "there is no healthier locality for lung, throat, or emphysema infections."

Three grand hotels, the Martin, the Brunswick, and the Medlock, all just steps from the depot, welcomed trainloads of guests, some arriving in fine Pullman cars. Local self-made millionaire Edward Buchanan was born an orphan and was adopted by Mr. and Mrs. Leslie Buchanan. Young Edward quit school after two years and went to work at the depot. A quick learner, Edward became an adept telegraph operator for Western Union, impressively receiving messages with his left hand while simultaneously tapping outgoing ones with his right hand. After traveling for Western Union for 10 years, he took a job as an operator at Hudson & Company, a Wall Street cotton brokerage. Buchanan moved up in the company, becoming a junior partner and enjoying inclusion in an elite circle of New York's wealthy, often living for months at the Waldorf Astoria Hotel with his wife, Bertie Redwine, a model and stunning beauty. Buchanan funded much of the early development of Norcross. He donated $1,000 in seed money to the ladies group to begin the first library; he established a waterworks and electrical plant, allowing neighbors to "hook on" for free; and he was known for giving clothing to newsboys in cold winters and donating money to the Uncle Remus Memorial Fund. He is also fondly remembered for offering children money to release june bugs when they held them by the legs with string. In a "rags to riches to rags again" story, Buchanan went bust after a stock scandal and died with only $60 in his bank account. The Methodist church, another one of his many causes, purchased the fine marker that graces his grave at the city cemetery.

Excitement accompanied the trains as they rolled in front of the depot, down the sidetrack, and alongside 7 Jones Street to load and unload livestock, bales of cotton, dry goods, and passengers. Norcross came alive at night when the brass band played in the shell at Thrasher Park, but by 1920, the thrill of the grass drew everyone over to the town ball field. All the shopkeepers closed their doors and everyone sat on the hillside looking over the sandlot behind the brick school on College Street when the Nuggets hosted games against other town teams. Norcross nurtured the talents of many fine players—in fact, in the 1920s, Norcross had more locals drafted to play professionally per capita than any other town in the United States. Especially notable are two sets of brothers, Red and Ivey Wingo and Roy and Cleo Carlyle. These hometown heroes played with the likes of Babe Ruth, Harry Heilmann, and another boy from Georgia, Ty Cobb. Roy Carlyle still holds the local record for the longest home run, a drive he smacked 618 feet. Ivey Wingo crouched behind the plate for the Cincinnati Reds when they won the 1919 World Series against the Chicago White Sox. Unfortunately, he was not able to enjoy the win, as it was a result of the famous "Black Sox" scandal, with Chicago throwing the series, resulting in Shoeless Joe Jackson's expulsion from baseball. In 2010, the Wingo brothers were inducted into the Gwinnett County Sports Hall of Fame at Cool Ray Stadium, home of the Atlanta Braves' AAA minor-league affiliate, the Gwinnett Braves. Ivey Wingo and Roy Carlyle are both interred at the city cemetery.

More recently, Norcross sports fans have cheered on Jodie Meeks, who led Norcross High School to its first state basketball championship in 2006, had a great collegiate career at the University of Kentucky, and now plays professionally for the Philadelphia 76ers. A 2007 Norcross graduate, Gani Lawal, starred at Georgia Tech and currently plays basketball in France.

Norcross is also proud of Chandler Massey, a 2009 graduate who was nominated for an Emmy for his portrayal of Will Horton on the soap opera *Days of Our Lives* in 2010, an indication of his blossoming acting career in Hollywood.

Now, as so many did then, visitors join locals in walking, strolling their children, or riding bikes into the historic but greatly revitalized Norcross proper, enjoying the many parks, shopping a variety of high-end stores, conducting business with state senators, attorneys, and insurance men, or enjoying ample offerings of fine food, fresh-brewed coffee, and a wide variety of entertainment.

CHAPTER 1

A Whistle-Stop of Many Wonders

Since the late 1800s, when the Airline Belle, a 20-mile-long commuter route, first brought folks back and forth from Atlanta, Norcross has been a whistle-stop of wonderment. Locals dressed up to watch the characters step off the train at the depot. Affluent city types rode out for a holiday, businessmen for trade, farmers to weigh cotton, Civil War veterans to have reunions, and teachers and preachers traveled to connect with students and parishioners on their Gwinnett County circuits. (Courtesy of Carl and Sherry Johnson.)

Abe Johnson's store, originally called Martin and Johnson, is the oldest store in town; today, it is Zapata's Restaurant. When Mr. Martin opened his own shop in 1899, each man would take turns filling large baskets to divide the goods. Shelves were stacked with bottles of Red Rock, Topp, and Mil-Kay colas and old copies of Grier's Almanac. A sign from the time period, still cherished by descendant Carl Johnson and his wife, Sherry, reads: "The store of three wonders: 1. You wonder if I have it, 2. I wonder where it is, 3. Everyone wonders how I find it." (Then image courtesy of Carl and Sherry Johnson.)

Between the second and third buildings of Martin and Johnson's general stores was a narrow alleyway where shopkeepers gathered around a stump of wood for serious games of checkers. In the early 1900s, teenager Reps Miller was guiding his father's wagonload of cotton over to the gin when something spooked the team while crossing the tracks and they bolted down the corridor. Soon after the dust, the game board, and the two startled gentlemen settled, a brick wall was constructed. (Then image courtesy of Carl and Sherry Johnson.)

Golden Garner, seen here, sold a variety of products from inside his Jones Street store. Bija Nucholls, the butcher, kept live hens in a cage behind the grocery store to assure costumers of a fresh chicken. The butcher would spin the birds around by the head until he heard the telltale crack of their neck, doing without modern electrical tools. In fact, while electricity came to Norcross in 1910, it was a luxury of the wealthy, not coming to most homes and businesses until the 1950s. (Then image courtesy of Carl and Sherry Johnson.)

Today, the old grocery store building houses Zapata's, a favorite drinking and eating spot whose entrance has changed very little since the time of the old store. Tacos, tortillas, and the best margaritas are now the fare. (Then image courtesy of Carl and Sherry Johnson.)

Dr. Sylvester Cain's father and mother, Sylvester and Maybelle Cain, operated this dry goods store in the building that originally housed McKenny's mercantile. The wood floors remain, but the walls, once stacked high with dry goods, now display fine art produced mostly by locals. Diners at Paizano's, the current occupant of the building, enjoy big bowls of pasta in the place that once sold pickles out of wooden barrels, flour out of gunnysacks, and whole cloth trimmed from bolts of fabric. (Then image courtesy of Evelyn Norman.)

The first brick building in Norcross was this standard railroad building at 7 Jones Street, built in 1890 by Riley Owen Medlock. A sidetrack, still beneath the sidewalk, ran alongside for the loading and unloading of large livestock, who were weighed on the big scales behind the building. It sat on the corner of Railroad Street, which was renamed Wingo Street in the 1950s. These days, locals pick up pizzas at Paizano's. The corner was squared off to allow for more seating within. (Then image courtesy of Evelyn Norman.)

The Norcross drugstore, directly next to Keady's drugstore, was home to Dr. Lietch's apothecary for many decades. So well loved was the doctor that when he took ill for some weeks, patients tidied his office space, which was above this storefront. In the 1950s, the shop became Thelma's Beauty Parlor. Today, Norcross residents can drop in to the barbershop for a haircut. (Then image courtesy of Carl and Sherry Johnson.)

Dr. W.M. Keady's drugstore on South Peachtree Street was opened in the early 1900s. Locals recall Keady as a sticking individual with a keen sense of humor. When the sheriff, pictured on the far left, mentioned he had an overflow of confiscated moonshine he needed to dump, the boys ran to gather mason jars to catch the corn mash at the end of the drain running down Skin Alley. Today, an attorney and a barber are in the two divided storefronts. (Then image courtesy of Carl and Sherry Johnson.)

Riley Owen Medlock built many of Norcross's solid structures, several of which still stand. Medlock had an office in Norcross as well as one in the Flat Iron Building in Atlanta, where he tragically fell down an open elevator shaft to his death in 1908. Today, attorney Gordon Tomlinson helps clients from his office space on South Peachtree Street. (Then image courtesy of Evelyn Norman.)

The Bank of Norcross (across the street, right) was established before 1900 by S.T. McElroy, Dr. Tom McDaniel, and Abe Johnson. Shortly after its move to this location in 1930, the bank was ordered closed for a federal "bank holiday," or government audit, which the bank took just 11 days to satisfy. In 1967, it became affiliated with Citizens and Southern Bank, or C&S. The building now houses an insurance agency. (Then image courtesy of Carl and Sherry Johnson.)

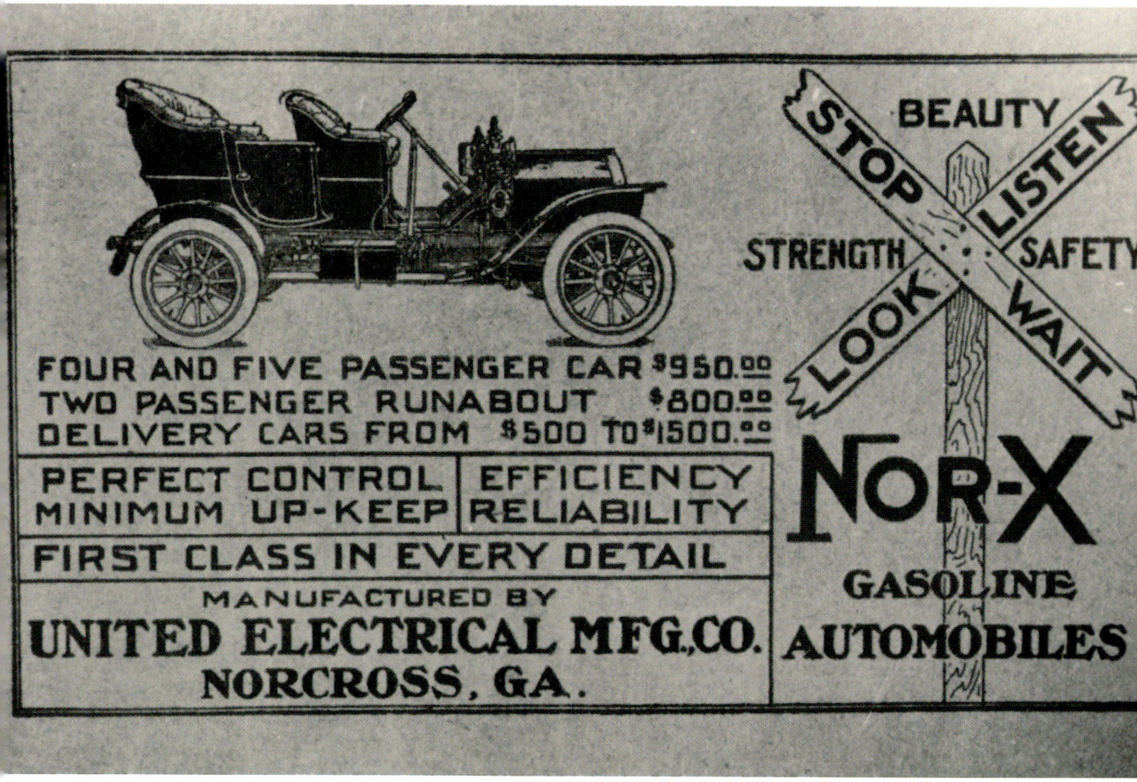

Edward Buchanan owned the first automobile manufacturing plant in Georgia here in Norcross. He produced the Nor-X—pronounced "Norcross"—a passenger car that sold for less than $500. It had to be retooled immediately after the first prototype rolled off the line, as the gears only worked in reverse. Today, worldwide sports equipment manufacturer Mizuno is headquartered in Norcross. (Then image courtesy of Carl and Sherry Johnson; now image courtesy of Mizuno.)

This postcard reads "Norcross on a buisy day," and the streets were indeed bustling with wagons full of cotton. Men sat or stood high atop the bales while driving their teams into town towards the gin behind these storefronts. A water well, directly in the center of the cross streets, once offered both men and horses a refreshing sip. (Then image courtesy of Carl and Sherry Johnson.)

Fine artist Florence Warbington Green painted homes and churches, as well as this streetscape, from her memories of the bustling downtown. Locals recall walking to town to purchase white bobby socks, farm implements, and freshly butchered meats. The original schoolhouse, up the hill in the center of the painting, was torn down, but many residents kept a brick from the old building. (Then image courtesy of Anita Andrews.)

In the 1950s, trains plowed through town but no longer made stops at the depot to unload people and goods. Norcross became a ghost town, as portrayed in this painting by Greg Jackson. Businesses shut down and storefronts sat empty until the early 1990s, when sidewalks were revitalized and blossoming trees were planted. Around the same time, the city council voted to allow the sale of alcohol, prompting the return of restaurants, followed by other businesses. (Then image courtesy of Greg Jackson Studios.)

This original freight depot burned to the ground in the late 1890s and was replaced by the present depot on the opposite side of the tracks, closer to the center of town. On his farm, which is now the property of the Atlanta Athletic Club, Homer Summerour cross-pollinated a hybrid half-and-half cotton which compressed from a 1,500-pound bundle into a 500-pound bale. Today, the McElroy family home sits roughly at the old location of the depot on Holcomb Bridge Road. (Then image courtesy of Carl and Sherry Johnson.)

The original Summerour cotton gin structure, which has been remodeled many times over the last 100 years, was located behind the storefronts of Jones Street. The yard of the gin was used as a setup spot for circus-type carnivals, complete with big bears and sideshows. Crowds witnessed a memorable shoot out there in the early 1900s when two local boys fought for the attentions of a female acrobat in town with a traveling troupe. (Then image courtesy of Carl and Sherry Johnson.)

In the 1950s, passenger trains no longer stopped at the depot and downtown businesses began moving to busy Buford Highway, just east of downtown. Paul Bolton worked at Garner's Garage, one of only two gas stations in Norcross, before working out a deal with the Garners, who constructed this building. Bolton's son Gene still runs a small shop there. The gas pumps and overhang were torn out when the road was widened in 1937. (Then image courtesy of Carl and Joan Garner.)

Folks dropped in to this shoe store twice a year for a new pair. In this photograph, the shopkeeper proudly displays the boxed items within a glass case. Today, the items may be different, but proprietors run several stores, including Good Things, the Purple Poppy, Antiques Traditions, Anna Balkan, and Home Norx, where Taylor Mackenzie Covert, seen here, offers shoppers handcrafted housewares, antiques, and jewelry. (Then image courtesy of Carl and Sherry Johnson.)

The Adams family operated a blacksmith shop at this location off of Skin Alley, a pathway behind South Peachtree Street, which has enjoyed recent revitalization and now features the Bleu House Fresh Market and Terra Dog Bakery. When Adams would leave Norcross on Tuesdays and Thursdays, his sons operated a moonshine still in the smith's shed, believing no one would pay any mind to the thick black smoke. (Then image courtesy of the Adams family.)

The grand, three-story Brunswick Hotel was noted for its quality food, including, according to an old advertisement, "Fine yellow legged chicken and not a hint of oleo margarine." Atlanta's wealthy would scoot out to Norcross to enjoy the clearer air and a classy meal. Woods Animal Hospital took over the brick post office building in the late 1970s and continues to serve the area's pet population. (Then image courtesy of James Woods.)

Lawrenceville had the first courthouse in Gwinnett County, built on January 15, 1821. The original courthouse on this site was burned to the ground by the Ku Klux Klan in 1871. A second was quickly built but was found unsafe and torn down in 1884. This two-story brick building, which has stood on the square since 1885, saw the lynching of many men and one woman. Today, more enjoyable events, like the wedding ceremony of Jeanette Kolacki, grace the grounds. (Then image courtesy of Evelyn Norman.)

CHAPTER 2

HITTING THE BOOKS

Education was highly regarded in Norcross, as evidenced by this advertisement for Norcross Public Schools dated September 15, 1899, which read in part: "All children between six and eighteen years old will be Pupils will be advanced as rapidly as consistent with thorough work. They will be expected, however, to master each study and stand a written examination on each book when it is finished." *Stickney's Speller*, *McGuffy's Readers*, *Grammar by Maxwell and Reed Kellog*, and *Sanford's Arithmetic* were among the early workbooks. (Courtesy of Sally Toole.)

This brick building, which housed grades 1–10 for whites, was built in 1910. It contained four rooms, with an upstairs auditorium used for plays, community events, and Saturday night movies. The belfry faced town and made for a striking landmark. On July 6, 1914, another brick building was built for $4,000. In the 1960s, the present-day school opened on Born Street about two blocks from this location. (Then image courtesy of Carl and Sherry Johnson.)

This sketch by an unknown artist of the first school, once located on College Street, was used on postcards. Many residents collected commemorative bricks when the building was deemed unsafe by the city in the 1950s and succumbed to the wrecking ball. In 1960, Norcross Elementary School opened its doors to all children, black and white, and state patrolmen lined the streets to prevent a disturbance, but the children were friendly and the morning began peacefully. (Then image courtesy of Jim Nesbit.)

The 1910 first-grade class had its photograph taken in front of the original brick school. Even at a young age, students would walk home at midday, sometimes as far as two miles from the schoolhouse, so their mothers could feed them lunch. In 1960, Norcross Elementary School, as a result of desegregation laws, welcomed children of all ethnicities. This first-grade class photograph from 1994–1995 reflects the modern town of Norcross. (Then image courtesy of Michelle Morgan; now image courtesy of William Toole.)

Competition between town baseball teams, like this 1946 team that included Edwin "Pop" Dean, faded in the 1950s, and school teams began drawing big crowds, as well as scouts. The 2001–2002 high school football team posed for its team photograph at the new field off of Spalding Drive, on property partially cleared by a tornado in 1998. (Then image courtesy of Norcross Old Timers Baseball Association; now image courtesy of Lily Toole.)

Edward Buchanan contributed $1,000 to the original library fund organized by the Norcross Woman's Club. Lola Key was the first librarian of the first library in Gwinnett County, working in the original building on North Peachtree Street for 19 years. A cornerstone, the contents of which are listed as a Confederate bill, an US flag, a Confederate flag, a silver coin, and a Bible, was laid in place on June 18, 1921, and refreshments were served. The library opened with 2,500 books on the shelves. (Then image courtesy of Kate Awtrey.)

Just as the first librarians organized the card files, today's librarians keep up with an ever-changing computerized system. Now, patrons can look up hard copies of books on the shelves and also access the internet from computer cubicles. In the old days, the library was quiet and children were shushed when they spoke too loudly, but today, the library bustles with activity and only a small reading room remains a quiet zone. (Then image courtesy of Norcross Public Library.)

Betty Wingo (left below) and another, unidentified librarian stand outside the library when it was housed on Carlyle Street in the 1960s. The community outgrew this building and the Lanier Regional Library System constructed a new building off Buford Highway. The Kudzu Art Zone occupies the space that was artist George Keener's studio from 1988 until shortly before his death in 2003. Today, Anne LeBaire (left above) and Dianna Rice (right above) offer art lessons and sells fine art at the studio. (Then image courtesy of Norcross Public Library.)

Self-made millionaire Edward Buchanan, a boy orphaned by his parents and reportedly taken in by the Tedder family after wandering the streets for a time, donated the initial $1,000 needed to start the first library. He built this home with granite quarried from Stone Mountain for his adoptive mother in 1910, making it completely modern with indoor plumbing and electricity. (Then image courtesy of Carl and Sherry Johnson.)

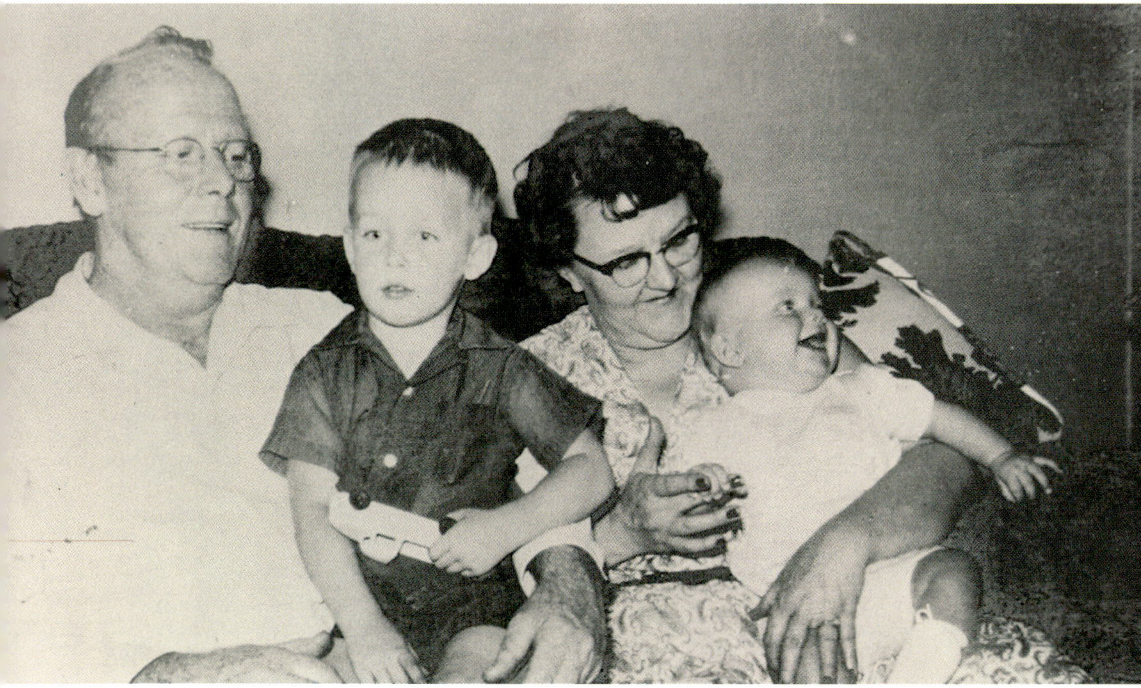

Absalom "Red" Wingo and his wife, Grace, play with their grandsons John and James in this 1954 family snapshot. Wingo and his brother, Ivey, were baseball stars in the 1920s and were inducted into the Gwinnett County Public Schools Hall of Fame in 2011 at Cool Ray Stadium, the home of the Gwinnett Braves. Posing at the induction ceremony are, from left to right, John Wingo; Ivey Wingo's granddaughter Michelle Morgan; Absalom "Abby" Wingo, named for his uncle; and James Wingo. (Then image courtesy of James Wingo; now image Courtesy of Sally Toole.)

CHAPTER 3

WAGONS, WHEELS, AND WHISTLES

Young Harry Nesbit pretends to fly in his toy airplane in the backyard. From early days when wagons carved out deep trenches in dirt paths to the nights when muscle cars drag-raced up and down Highway 141, one of two busy thoroughfares bypassing the historic district, wheels of all makes and models have rolled through Norcross. (Courtesy of Jim Nesbit.)

Jeff Bolton is gently restoring this 1951 Farmall Cub tractor, which his family used for decades to farm much of the land they owned on both sides of Interstate 85. That land now includes Beaver Ridge Elementary School, a CarMax showroom, and a large home improvement store. The tractor is now on family land in Hoschton and enjoyed by Jeff Bolton (sitting), his son, Dakota, and Ross Bolton. (Then and now images courtesy of Jeff Bolton.)

H.C. Suddereth purchased this Hudson Super Six new on October 13, 1947, for his wife. Since it was parked in 1963 with 30,170 miles on the odometer, a pair of lady's gloves, a grocery list noting her need for a can of tuna, a box of crackers, and a tin of Aspergum have sat on the dash. David Jackson is currently restoring the old beauty and foresees it back on the road as a highlight of the 2012 Norcross Car Show. (Then and now images courtesy of David Jackson.)

Although the trees have grown, the road is paved, and the houses have been remodeled many times over, these homes, built before 1900 on Thrasher Street, have not changed that much. This busy little road leads visitors directly into town from Holcomb Bridge Road, as it did in the late 1800s for farmers coming into town from the Chattahoochee River. (Then image courtesy of Evelyn Norman.)

Since its incorporation in 1870, the streets of Norcross have always been full of visitors, the first of whom arrived in horse-drawn wagons. Since 1997, hundreds of visitors delight every year at the annual car show, which began as a fundraising event to pay the mounting medical bills of Kristi DeLeon, who suffered fatal injuries in a car accident. The car show now distributes scholarships in DeLeon's name. (Then image courtesy of Carl and Sherry Johnson.)

The train depot was originally built on the western side of the tracks, but a contract dated July 23, 1896, calls for its relocation across the tracks on August 6 of that same year. However, it was not moved until 1909, when John P. Pettyjohn was contracted by the Southern Railway to do the work, moving it to the east of the tracks for a sum of $4,750. (Then image courtesy of Carl and Sherry Johnson.)

This eastern view shows the depot before the drastic 1990s remodeling job that allowed for a new restaurant to open inside. At this time, the depot was not much more than a storage barn for the city's public works. The depot structure is still owned by the railroad, which also holds property rights to all land approximately 20 feet on both sides of all usable tracks. Two rails are seen here, but only one remains in use. (Then image courtesy of Carl and Sherry Johnson.)

Railroad work gangs lived in tent houses along what was then Railroad Street from the late 1890s well into the 1930s. These employees from Norcross likely rode the route from the Atlanta terminal all the way northward to Washington, DC, checking for tramps stowed away in the boxcars or snagging bags of mail or cash at depots along the way. (Then image courtesy of Carl and Sherry Johnson.)

Several crossings in town have been closed as a result of accidents, including a fatal one involving a family. Shirley Letson recalls playing in the culvert drain when this wreck occurred in the 1930s. Today, truckers sometimes fail to heed posted warnings and continue to cause accidents at the crossings. (Then image courtesy of Evelyn Norman; now image courtesy of Lily Toole.)

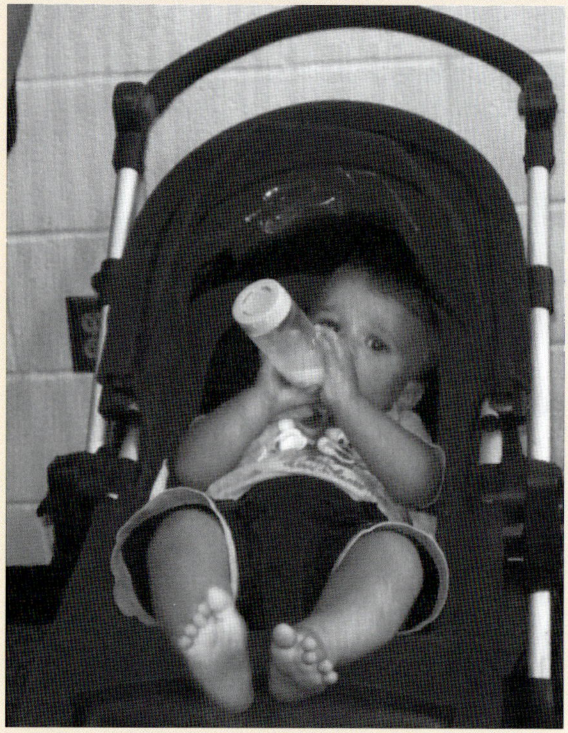

This old wicker carriage, with an unidentified baby, was quite an expensive item when it was purchased new some time prior to 1940 and would now be considered a vintage antique. Norcross boasts several tree-canopied parks that attract young families, like that of young Noah Lynch, who can wheel in to shop, eat, and relax. (Then image courtesy of Jim Nesbit; now image courtesy of Sally Toole.)

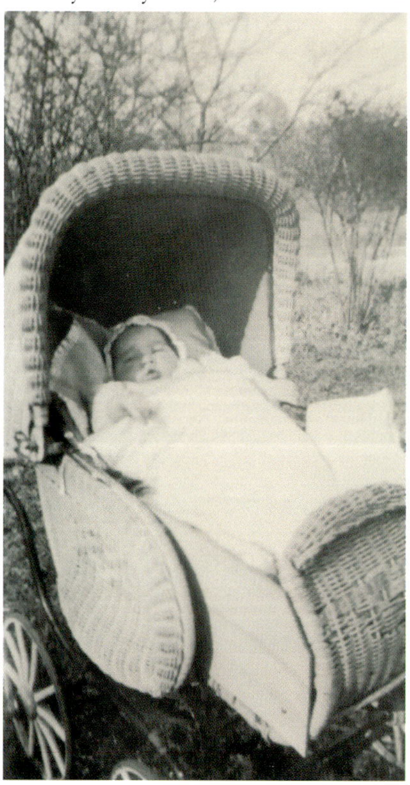

CHAPTER 4

PARKS AND RECREATION

Baseball was the best entertainment in Norcross, and everyone gathered at the open lot below the old schoolhouse to watch the town team. For many years, baseball was just about all there was to do, so businesses closed and folks walked to the sandlot. Brothers Ivey and Red Wingo grew up in a house next to the field and both played major league baseball in the 1920s. (Courtesy of James Wingo.)

Dodson Park was renamed Thrasher Park by a unanimous city council vote on January 1, 1934. For a time, a building north of the pavilion was referred to as the courthouse and was used as a "mayor's court" by L.H. Letson, but after a review of Thrasher's stipulations that this area never be used for industrial purposes, the building was torn down. The park now hosts various forms of entertainment, including concerts, just as it did in the late 1890s. (Then image courtesy of Carl and Sherry Johnson.)

Evelyn "Bud" Norman gets a twinkle in her eye when recalling long summer days spent scooting around town on skates or bicycles. The gang would play the arm-breaking-train game, where several children would hook arms and run full speed down the sidewalk in the center of the park. Every Tuesday from spring to fall, the Whistle Stop Farmer's Market offers special events, like this visit from Shauna Smith of the North Georgia Petting Zoo, who brought the first kangaroo to ever be at the park. (Then image courtesy of Carl and Sherry Johnson.)

Originally an empty lot used as the school athletic field, this baseball field helped four boys from Norcross fulfill their dream of playing in the big leagues. The park was named for longtime Norcross mayor Lillian Webb. In the 2000s, a public park complete with fountains and a large open green space have replaced the baseball field. (Then image courtesy of Sally Toole.)

Kevin Dunn, leader of Norcross Boy Scout Troop 26, explains this photograph of two unidentified Scouts, saying, "The boy on the right appears to have just had his Eagle pinned over his pocket and the rank on his sleeve signifies a patrol leader. It was likely taken between the two World Wars, probably around 1930, due to the type of leggings worn." Modern-day Star Scout Will Thomas (left) and Eagle Scout Andrew Dunn strike the same pose as their Scout predecessors. (Then image courtesy of Michelle Morgan.)

From the early 1880s until the Great Depression, Norcross was considered a resort town, and the Brunswick Hotel offered guests wraparound porches on all of its three stories. Many relaxed in the rockers sipping a Coca-Cola, but not on Sundays, when it was illegal in Norcross. Today, Woods Animal Hospital is a popular veterinarian's office. (Then image courtesy of James Woods.)

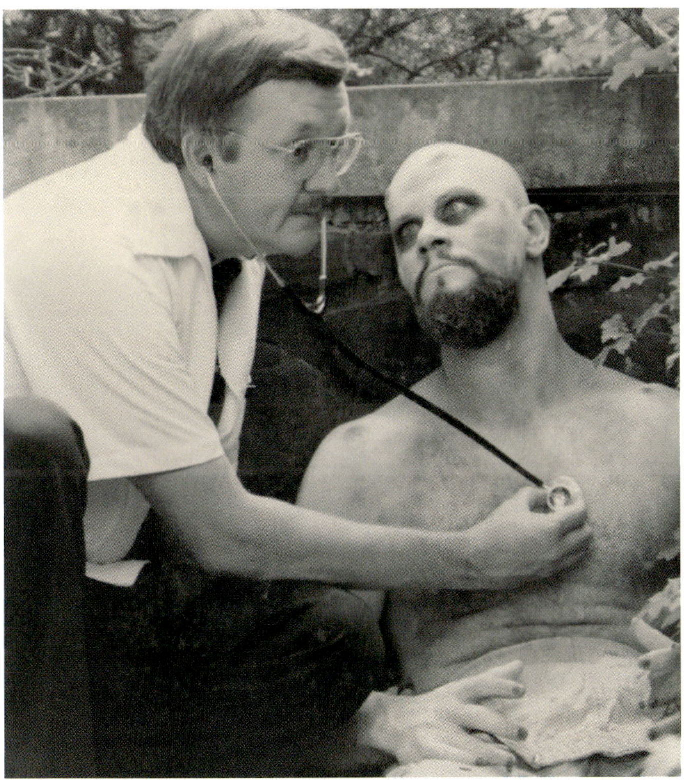

Veterinarian James Woods welcomed Hollywood into his animal hospital in 1983 and is seen here joking around with a character from the film *The Mutant*. Today, Norcross still hosts commercial and movie filming, as well as offering History Walks of Norcross, led by costumed guides like Winnie Sue Simpson. (Then image courtesy of James Woods.)

One of three hotels in town, the Medlock Hotel sat on the corner of Thrasher Street and Holcomb Bridge Road. Later, the Medlock family took the hotel apart and used the wood to build a family home across the street. Both structures are now gone, but the empty lot shows how close to the dirt road—which remained unpaved until the 1950s—the hotel once sat. (Then image courtesy of Evelyn Norman.)

The first pool in Gwinnett County was dug by hand behind the home of Connie Warbington, shown here in the 1950s, off of Holcomb Bridge Road. Some of the stones that once lined the perimeter are visible near the spring-fed creek that once filled it. Folks paid 10¢ to swim here all day. (Then image courtesy of Bob Warbington.)

In 2007, the Norcross Baseball Old Timers Association, some of whom played on the town's Nuggets teams of the 1960s, gathered to rededicate their collection of memorabilia under the stairwell at city hall. Below, in 2011, Michelle Morgan and James Wingo greet association member Carl Garner. (Then and now images courtesy of Sally Toole.)

Atlanta Athletic Club member Bill Hirsch volunteered as a marshal at the Highlands Course during the 1981 Professional Golf Association (PGA) Championship, raising his arms to quiet the crowd as each player teed off on the sixth hole. Anthony Holwill performed the same task 30 years later when the championship returned in August 2011. Keegan Bradley won that 93rd PGA championship, following in the footsteps of David Toms, who won there in 2001, and Raymond Floyd, who claimed the coveted Wannamaker Cup in 1981. (Then image courtesy of Sally Hirsch Toole; now image courtesy of Jennifer Holwill.)

From 1870 to well into the 1960s, most Norcross children had too many chores to play much. Milking cows was just one chore of young Tillie Bolton, shown here on his family's farm. In the earliest days, livestock is said to have roamed freely around town, but now the only cow people see is this statue that guards the garden of resident John Landstrom along South Peachtree Street. (Then image courtesy of Jeff Bolton.)

CHAPTER 5

MILITARY AND MUNICIPAL

Early forms of communication included the telegraph and the town telephone line. Operators connected calls by plugging a limited number of wires into bulky switchboxes like this one. During both world wars, families communicated only via the postal service, dreading the receipt of telegrams, which often brought tragic news. (Courtesy of Carl and Sherry Johnson.)

The first post office was a wooden structure at 45 South Peachtree Street that burned. In the 1950s, it was replaced with this brick building. When the community outgrew this little building, the current post office was built along Mitchell Street. (Then image courtesy of Carl and Sherry Johnson.)

The first city hall housed a single jail cell, the fire department's one garage door, the council and mayor's office, and a single clerk for the collection of utility payments. Today's two-story building houses the same services but with much more square footage. Each Christmas season, a spiral staircase has enough room for a large lit tree to delight residents. (Then image courtesy of Carl and Sherry Johnson.)

Confederate veterans held annual reunions on the porch of the Medlock Hotel in the 1890s, sharing recollections of the War Between the States. In 2009, the Veterans of Foreign Wars gathered once again on Memorial Day to honor the fallen and reminisce and share war stories. Veteran Les Young (first row, far right) and retired Air Force colonel John Adams (first row, second from right) are seen above in 2009. (Then image courtesy of Evelyn Norman; now image courtesy of Sally Toole.)

Camp Gordon rifle range was an extension of the Air Corps 10 miles south of Norcross. Men practiced sharp-shooting into the hill just beyond the high wires of today's Georgia Power electrical transformers. Sheffield Forest subdivision was built on much of the land after World War II. (Then image courtesy of Carl and Sherry Johnson.)

Many sons of Norcross were lost in both world wars. This soldier, believed to be Curtis Nesbit, takes a moment with his young son upon his return home. The citizens of Norcross have set an admirable example of municipal and military service to the city and to the country. Below, Norcross police officer Russell Knox gives his son, Micah, a big hug during a community event on April 28, 2011. (Then image courtesy of Jim Nesbit.)

The first fire response in Norcross was no more than a shed, a water wagon, and an alarm system near the site of Gwinnett County Fire Station No. 1. To report an emergency, one had to smash the small window of the door, reach in to turn the knob, and switch on a siren, which blasted closer to town. For several years, the station was located on College Street near the old ball field. (Then image courtesy of the Norcross Welcome Center.)

Early on, all in-town homes drew water from wells, just as the farmhouses did. This well, still on Thrasher Street, provided water to the Brunswick Hotel. In 1910, the first water towers was constructed, but it was many decades before the average home had indoor plumbing. Well diggers were kept busy hand-digging many wells, the relics of which can be spotted around town. (Then image courtesy of Carl and Sherry Johnson.)

During the time he served the town as sheriff, Garland Sexton also delivered milk in the 1950s and 1960s. His car is seen here parked behind his home on Lake Drive, where he lived for 50 years. Sexton's home was later demolished, and a new home was built. Today, police officers patrol the streets on foot, on bicycles, and from behind the wheel of an SUV, a Ford Mustang, and several cruisers. They also have a well-trained K-9 unit. (Then image courtesy of Garland Sexton.)

Dr. Oliver Oglethorpe Simpson, one of the first mayors of Norcross, also practiced medicine from his home on North Peachtree Street. Bucky Johnson, the longtime Georgia Technical College band director, has held the office for two terms, having beaten out longtime mayor Lillian Webb in a runoff election in 2008. (Then image courtesy of Carl and Sherry Johnson.)

CHAPTER 6

A Fine Feeling of Family and Fellowship

John Stapp and his wife, Julie, were, like most early Norcross residents, self-sufficient farmers. This farm in the Beaver Ruin settlement is part of an area that became Interstate 85. (Then image courtesy of Jeff Bolton.)

On the afternoon of May 17, 1872, a group of 17 people, including Jonathan Thrasher and his brother David, gathered "In His Name" at the one-room Community House to discuss building a church on a corner lot just southwest of Thrasher Park. Believers there were dipped in Johnson's Lake off of Barton Street until a steam-heat baptismal was installed. The Baptist congregation held the first service at its current location in 1963. (Then image courtesy of Carl and Sherry Johnson.)

The congregation of what is now Norcross Methodist Church dates farther back than any other in the area. Beginning before the Civil War, Flint Hill Primitive Church was located south of Norcross proper. Disintegrating tombstones are said to hold the death dates of early settlers from the 1800s. The church moved to Beaver Ruin Road in the 1970s. The Lionheart Theatre Company now makes its home in the historic 1872 church sanctuary at 10 College Street. (Then image courtesy of Evelyn Norman.)

Hopewell Baptist Church was started by several families of recently freed slaves who were given parcels of land in the Norcross vicinity as a part of the Emancipation Proclamation. After a fire in the 1920s, a reorganized congregation began building this granite structure in 1947 from stones quarried out of Stone Mountain, where the Ku Klux Klan used to hold meetings. The current megachurch draws parishioners from all across metropolitan Atlanta. (Then and now images courtesy of Kate Awtrey.)

The Presbyterian church's congregation outgrew this structure, moving to its current location along Medlock Bridge Road. The old building still hosts Hispanic services below this ominously leaning steeple. Above, Linda Leece walks her dogs all around the historic district, where she lives. (Then image courtesy of Carl and Sherry Johnson.)

In 1928, Noah and Kate Adams and their son, John Guthrie Adams, moved to a home on Cemetery Street, farming the land where some Adamses are buried in Wright's Cemetery. John A. Adams, Noah's father, lived at 75 College Avenue, where they raised and sold chickens in a large coop. Today, several members of the Adams family run the Bleu House Market at 65 College Street as well as a cafe at 108 Cemetery Street (renamed Holcomb Bridge Road North in 2011). (Then image courtesy of the Adams family.)

Lou Bolton's kitchen, pictured above in August 1958, was modern in its day, but the old stove and table and chairs would be antique prizes today. The Bleu House Market's kitchen has all the modern amenities and prepares gourmet brunch, lunch, and popular picnic packs. (Then image courtesy of Jeff Bolton.)

Evelyn "Bud" Norman and her husband, Ralph, bought this house at 297 South Peachtree Street. Ralph knew that Bud loved the home, having played in its underpinnings as a child, and when it went up for auction, he bought it. Below, their son Bill poses with his mother while helping around the house. (Then image courtesy of Evelyn Norman.)

The Flint Hill plantation, now an events facility, was the early homestead of the family of Stephen T. McElroy, a Confederate veteran who lost a leg in the Civil War but returned to the emerging Norcross area to flourish as the owner of many businesses. (Courtesy of Carl and Sherry Johnson.)

This striking, one-of-a-kind home on Born Street was built for the Ivy family and was repainted in an old-fashioned style in 2011. It has been very well kept. (Then image courtesy of Carl and Sherry Johnson.)

Mount Carmel Methodist Church, outside of the downtown district of Norcross, was the first congregation for early settlers. Its cemetery is a historical landmark featuring the gravesite of the first white baby born in this part of Georgia. The Methodists gather outside each year for a large homecoming meal. (Then image courtesy of Jeff Bolton.)

This house was the first in town with a grand Victorian floorplan. It was so striking that it made many well-to-do neighbors jealous, and four more homes were built with the same layout. The prominent families of Norcross hosted grand parties in these attractive homes, all of which still stand. (Then image courtesy of Carl and Sherry Johnson.)

In order to keep the five Victorian homes just a little different from each another, the builder added an additional room to each as the construction progressed, so this home, the last one, has four more rooms than the first one had. (Then image courtesy of Carl and Sherry Johnson.)

The Rochester House, with its extreme roof pitch, overlooks Thrasher Park at the corner of Jones and North Peachtree Streets. Hollis Rochester was a fine young athlete whose body was found near the tracks just south of the depot. The details of his untimely death remain a mystery. Today, Cindy Flynn's cat, Ava, is often seen enjoying the view from the front window. (Then image courtesy of Michelle Morgan.)

For more than 140 years, the swings in Thrasher Park have offered a cool respite from the summer heat. This little girl is thought to be Anna Lisa, a spirit detected by a local paranormal team who investigates local haunts each October for History Walks of Norcross. Swinging is still a favorite pastime for Lisa A. Owens and Xander Cole Woodellboth. (Then image courtesy of the authors' collection, from an unknown source.)

The Johnson and Rochester families sought relief from the Georgia summer on Simpson family land along the Chatahoochee River. In those days, people loaded food, chairs, tables, china, and silverware into wagons and rolled down to the banks of the chilly river. Today, folks bring coolers and jackets to enjoy Jones Bridge Park in the wintertime. (Then image courtesy of Michelle Morgan.)

This bridge over the Chatahoochee River was instrumental in growing commerce and industry in Norcross from 1900 to the 1940s. It replaced the ferry system that was in use from 1820 to 1890. The Gwinnett County side of the bridge was torn down and sold to the federal government for scrap metal to help the war effort. (Then image courtesy of Carl and Sherry Johnson.)

Martha and Sue Simpson were born premature on a cold January day in 1918 in the home their grandfather, Oliver Oglethorpe Simpson, at 297 North Peachtree Street. Neighbors chopped wood for the fireplace and they were nursed to strength in a small room in the back. Martha cherished this quilt, which the Simpsons were given upon their settlement in the area around 1820. Martha died in that same small room in the back on a cold January day in 2009. (Then image courtesy of Jim Nesbit.)

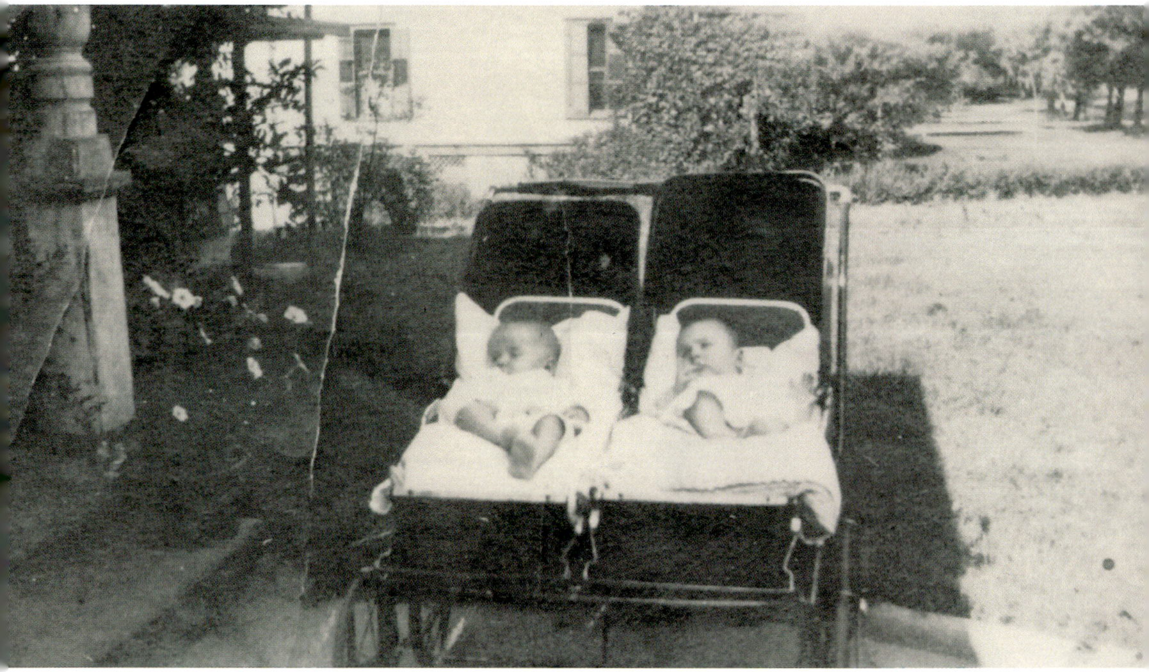

Martha Simpson Nesbit's husband, Curtis, died suddenly in his sleep and was buried at the family's plot in the city cemetery. The stone structure stoically watches over the graves of so many Norcross residents. Martha, a beloved teacher at Summerour Middle School, is now interred next to her husband on this hillside above the youth football fields she could see from her classroom. (Then image courtesy of Jim Nesbit.)

Jeff Bolton stands behind one of his family's plots in the cemetery of Mount Carmel Methodist Church, the first congregation in the area. Jeff's grandfather, Tullis, stood at the same spot decades earlier. This historic graveyard is the final resting place for six generations of Boltons, who claimed area land they had won in the lottery of 1820. (Then image courtesy of Jeff Bolton.)

The Norcross City Cemetery sits atop a gentle hill with a beautiful view of the old Methodist church's steeple, restored in 2011. In autumn, the air is filled with the sound of football games, played just below the rusting wrought iron fences and the weathering headstones honoring those who called this little Southern railroad town home. (Then image courtesy of Jim Nesbit.)

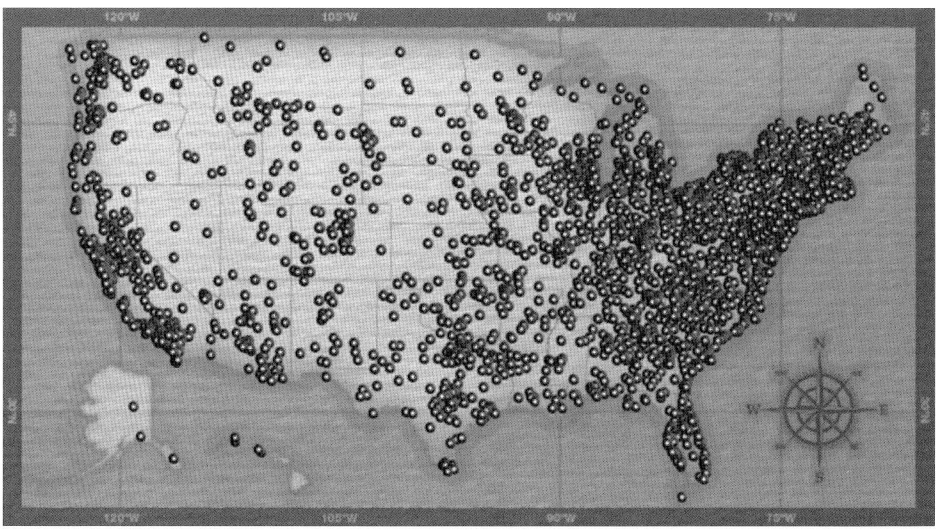

Consistent with our mission to preserve history on a local level, this book was printed in South Carolina on American-made paper and manufactured entirely in the United States. Products carrying the accredited Forest Stewardship Council (FSC) label are printed on 100 percent FSC-certified paper.

MADE IN THE USA